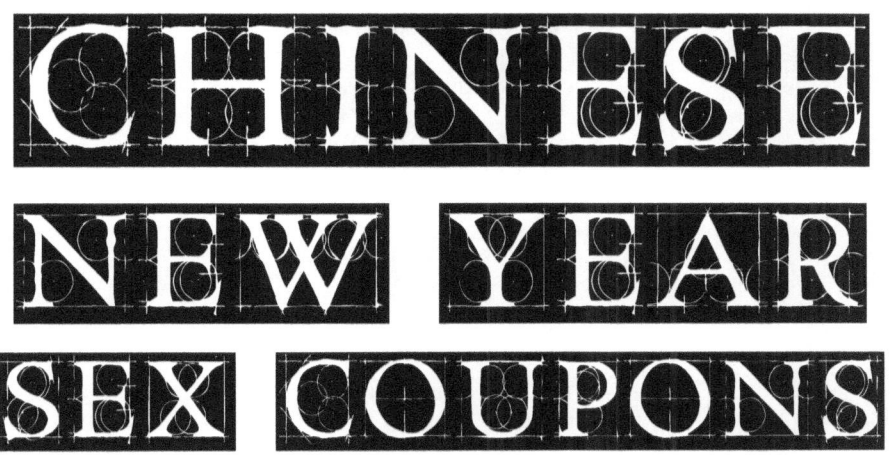

CHINESE NEW YEAR SEX COUPONS

I0417446

By: Lew Wah Ling

Tear Out The Coupons To Redeem

This coupon is for one morning quickie before work.

Back Side Of Coupon

This coupon is for sex in the bathroom looking in the mirror.

Back Side
Of Coupon

This coupon is for one week everyday of blow jobs.

Next week it is one week of oral pleasure for her in return everyday for a week.

Back Side
Of Coupon

Doggystyle sex watching Tv

Back Side
Of Coupon

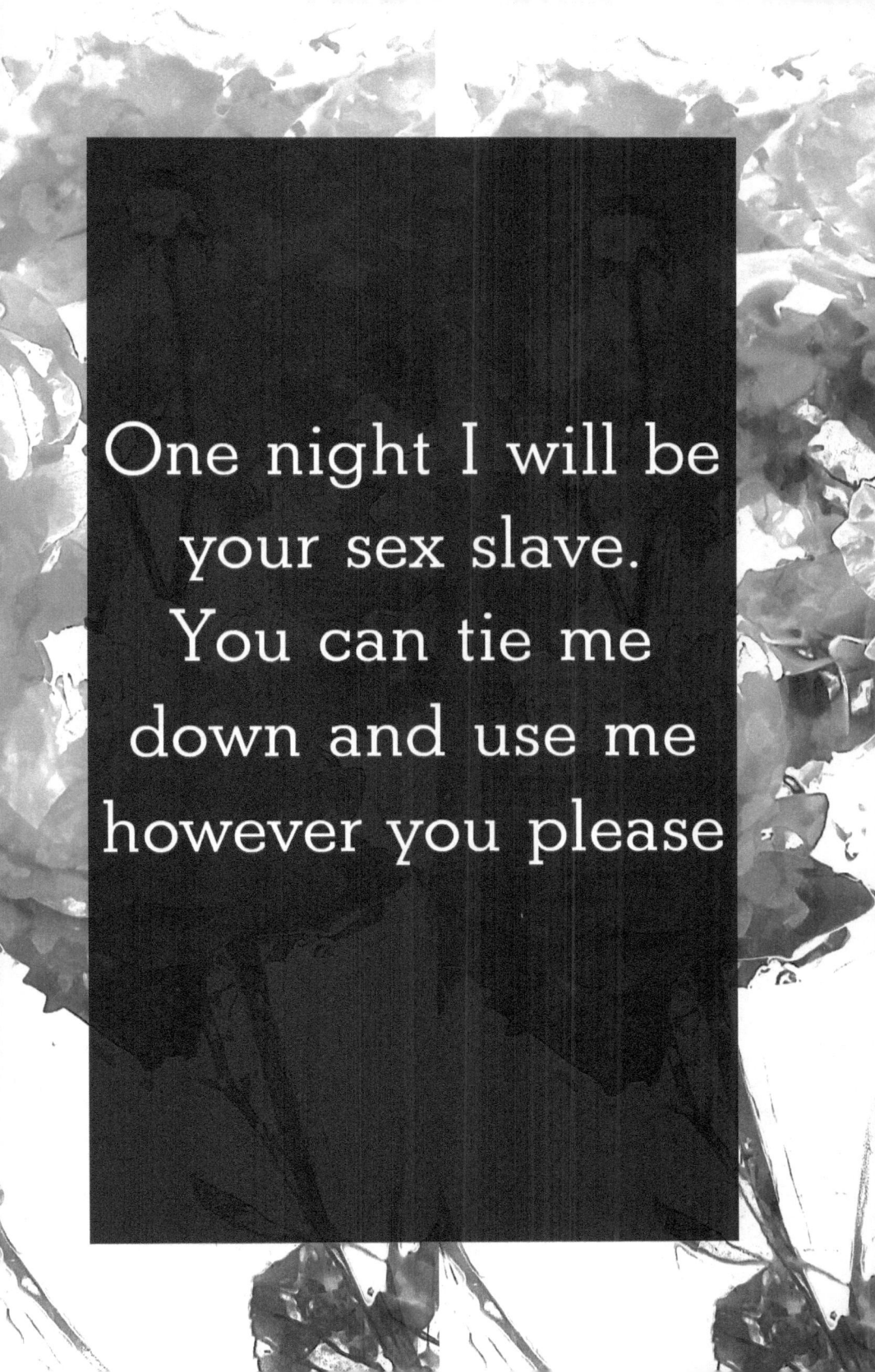

Back Side
Of Coupon

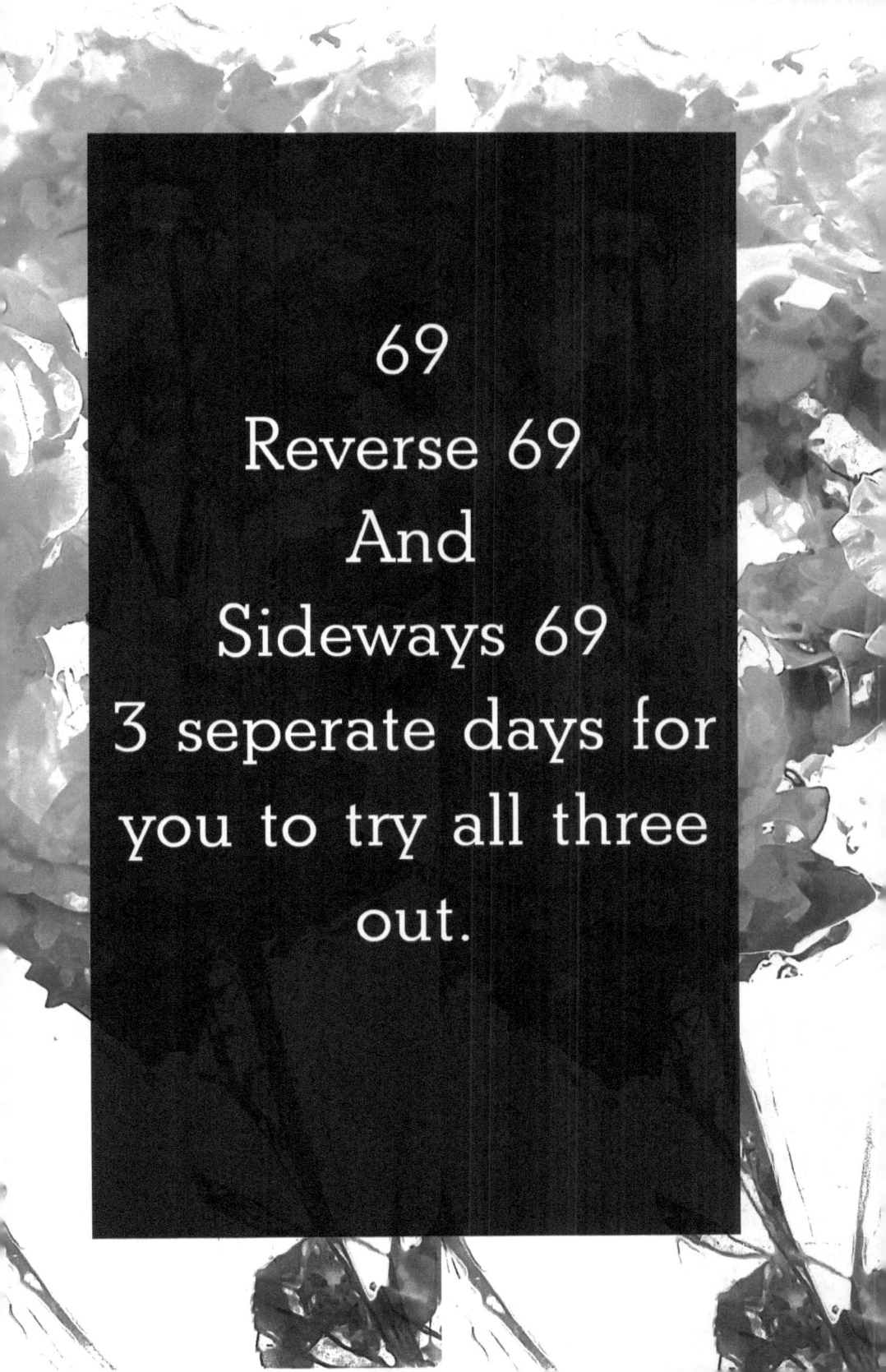

69
Reverse 69
And
Sideways 69
3 seperate days for
you to try all three
out.

Back Side Of Coupon

With a vibrting bullet tie her down to the bed and use it on her for an hour, than switch where you place the vibrator on his balls and blow/ have sex with him.

Back Side
Of Coupon

45 minute massage for her with oil. During the last ten minutes of the massage she must suck his cock, while he fingers her.

Back Side Of Coupon

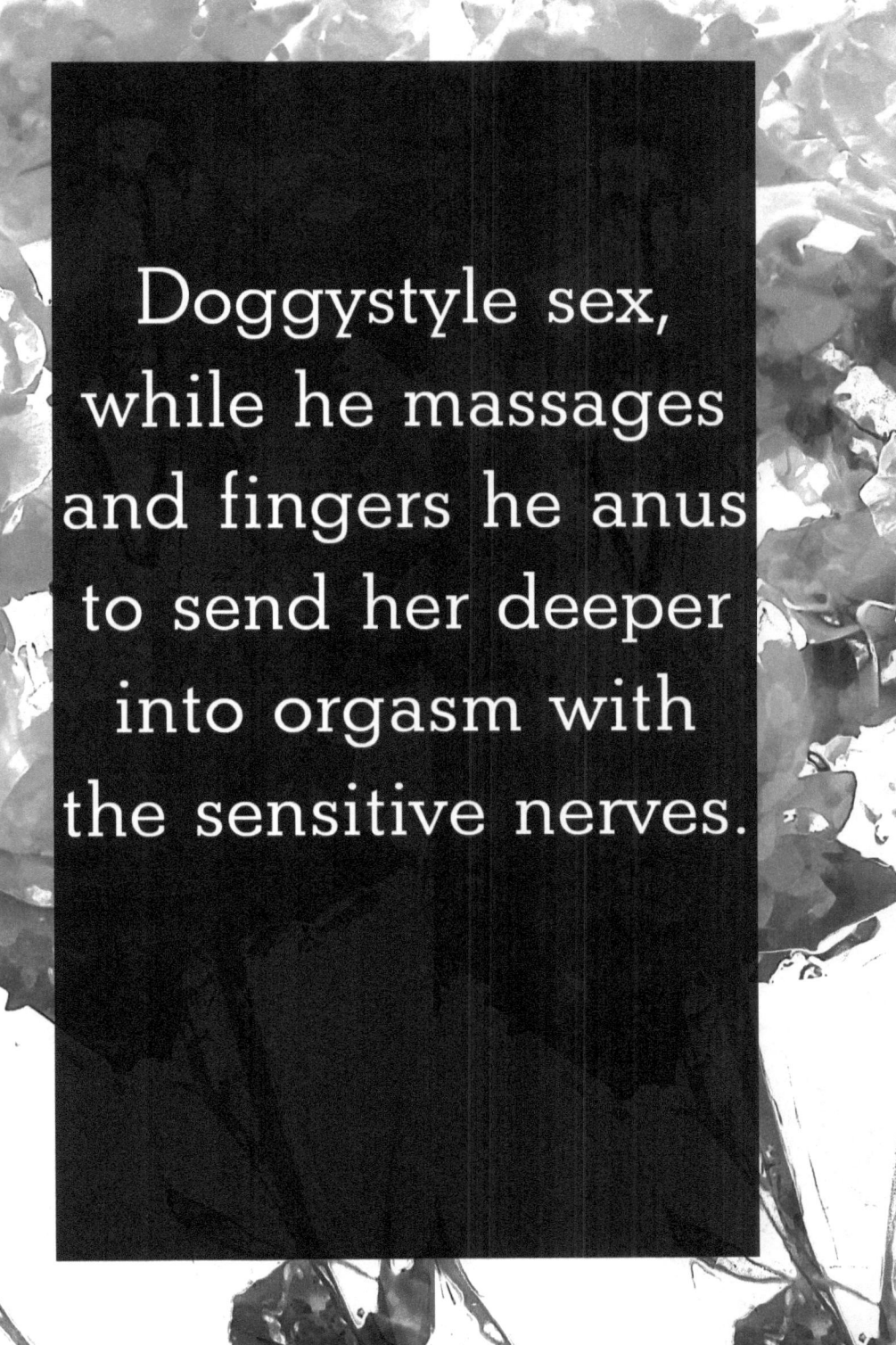

Doggystyle sex, while he massages and fingers he anus to send her deeper into orgasm with the sensitive nerves.

Back Side
Of Coupon

She must masterbate to orgasm in front of you. If she is uncomfortable she can suck your cock while masterbating.

Back Side Of Coupon

She has to put on her sexiest outfit and he will take pictures and have sex with her in his favorite position

Back Side
Of Coupon

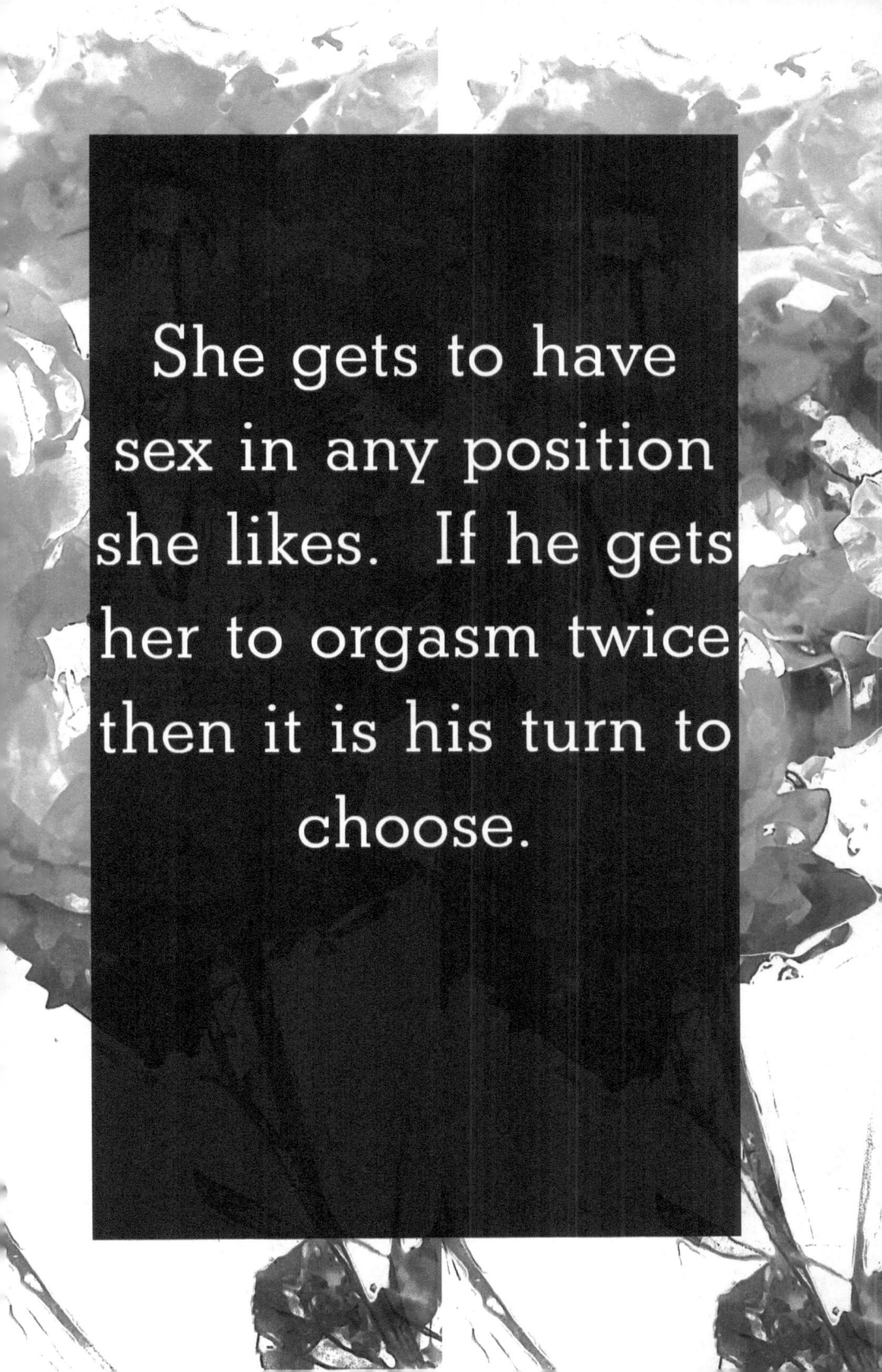

She gets to have sex in any position she likes. If he gets her to orgasm twice then it is his turn to choose.

Back Side Of Coupon